JUMPIN' JIM'S
CAMP
UKULELE

Compiled and Arranged by Jim Beloff

P9-BHZ-723

Foreword... 2
Chord Cabin... 3
First Aid 4
The Story of the Ukulele 59

SONGS
The Ants Go Marching................................. 6
The Bear Went Over The Mountain................. 8
Bingo 10
Camp Ukulele.. 12
Clementine... 14
The Climbing Song 16
Down By The Riverside 18
Down In The Valley 17
Erie Canal 20
Go Down, Moses 22
Happy Trails 24
Hello Mudduh, Hello Fadduh 26
He's Got The Whole World In His Hands.......... 29
Home On The Range................................... 30
I've Been Working On The Railroad 32
Kookaburra 34
Kum-Bah-Yah... 35
The Lion Sleeps Tonight 36
Michael, Row The Boat Ashore..................... 39
Oh, Susanna 40
On Top Of Old Smoky................................. 42
On Top Of Spaghetti.................................. 43
Puff, The Magic Dragon.............................. 44
Red River Valley 46
Rise And Shine... 47
She'll Be Coming 'Round The Mountain........... 48
Shenandoah... 49
Simple Gifts 54
The Sloop John B. 50
Swing Low, Sweet Chariot........................... 52
Take Me Out To The Ballgame 56
Taps... 72
Tell Me Why.. 58
This Land Is Your Land 60
This Old Man 55
Very Early Morning 62
Waltzing Matilda 66
The Water Is Wide..................................... 68
When The Saints Go Marching In 65
You Are My Sunshine.................................. 70

Copyright © 2000 FLEA MARKET MUSIC, INC.

HAL•LEONARD®

7777 W. BLUEMOUND RD. P.O. BOX 13819 MILWAUKEE, WI 53213

Edited by Ronny S. Schiff
Cover and Art Direction by Elizabeth Maihock Beloff
Graphics and Music Typography by Charylu Roberts

GREETINGS

........*Welcome to Camp Ukulele! We've been waiting for you! The canoes are pulled up on the lakeshore, the hammocks are swaying in the breeze, the lemonade is cold and the coals in the campfire are perfect for marshmallows. All that's missing is you and your uke to complete the picture.......*

In the course of working on this book, I conjured up a lot of old summer camp memories. Not all of them were wonderful, but a couple of nice ones do stand out. One was a crush I had on a girl named Ellen. At the last big campfire of the summer, she gave me a gum wrapper chain that I thought was about the greatest thing I'd ever gotten from anyone. Another standout was a counselor who played the guitar and encouraged my own playing.

Unlike the real thing, but maybe better, Camp Ukulele is a state of mind. A place that doesn't exist on a map but suddenly appears, Brigadoon-like, wherever the songs in this book are sung and strummed by a family, a group of friends or anyone swinging in a hammock on a lazy summer day. What is also nice is that most of these songs are very easy to play, proving that you only need to know three or four chords to play lots of songs. Perhaps that is part of their appeal. They are simple and yet have lyrics and melodies so memorable and durable that they get passed on from generation to generation.

A lot of former campers helped us with this book. Special thanks for song suggestions and personal camping photographs to Marv and "Mike" Beloff, Jimmy Dugan, Don Maihock, Sally Shernow, Ronny Schiff, Gary Shrager and Eileen Sullivan, Ginny Stevens, Peter Thomas and Eric Weinberger. Also a big thank you for the fun "song audition" night to Larry Dilg, Mimi Kennedy, Phyllis and Dale Webb and Peter Wingerd. Thanks, as always, to Charylu Roberts, Wendy DeWitt, Ronny Schiff for all that you do. An extra special thank you to Liz Beloff who envisioned, named and art-directed this songbook. Your wonderful fingerprints are all over this! Finally, the biggest thank you to you who are enjoying this book. Here's wishing you many pleasant hours, days, weeks and years strumming at "Camp Ukulele!"

—Jumpin' Jim
Los Angeles, CA 2000

Also Available: (Books) *Jumpin' Jim's Ukulele Favorites; Jumpin' Jim's Ukulele Tips 'N' Tunes; Jumpin' Jim's Ukulele Gems; Jumpin' Jim's Ukulele Christmas; Jumpin' Jim's '60s Uke-In; Jumpin' Jim's Gone Hawaiian; The Ukulele: A Visual History.* **(CDs)** *Jim's Dog Has Fleas; For the Love of Uke; Legends of Ukulele; It's a Fluke* **(Video)** *The Joy of Uke.*

Visit us on the web at www.fleamarketmusic.com

CHORD CABIN

Tune Ukulele
G C E A

MAJOR CHORDS

A | A♯ / B♭ | B | C | C♯ / D♭ | D | D♯ / E♭ | E | F | F♯ / G♭ | G | G♯ / A♭

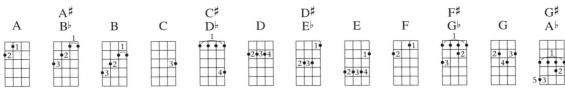

MINOR CHORDS

Am | A♯m / B♭m | Bm | Cm | C♯m / D♭m | Dm | D♯m / E♭m | Em | Fm | F♯m / G♭m | Gm | G♯m / A♭m

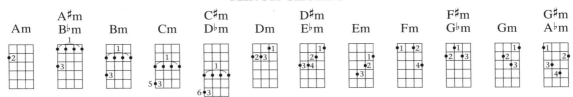

DOMINANT SEVENTH CHORDS

A7 | A♯7 / B♭7 | B7 | C7 | C♯7 / D♭7 | D7 | D♯7 / E♭7 | E7 | F7 | F♯7 / G♭7 | G7 | G♯7 / A♭7

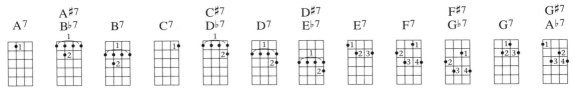

MINOR SEVENTH CHORDS

Am7 | A♯m7 / B♭m7 | Bm7 | Cm7 | C♯m7 / D♭m7 | Dm7 | D♯m7 / E♭m7 | Em7 | Fm7 | F♯m7 / G♭m7 | Gm7 | G♯m7 / A♭m7

DIMINISHED SEVENTH CHORDS (dim)

Adim | A♯dim / B♭dim | Bdim | Cdim | C♯dim / D♭dim | Ddim | D♯dim / E♭dim | Edim | Fdim | F♯dim / G♭dim | Gdim | G♯dim / A♭dim

AUGMENTED FIFTH CHORDS (aug or +)

Aaug | A♯aug / B♭aug | Baug | Caug | C♯aug / D♭aug | Daug | D♯aug / E♭aug | Eaug | Faug | F♯aug / G♭aug | Gaug | G♯aug / A♭aug

3

FIRST AID

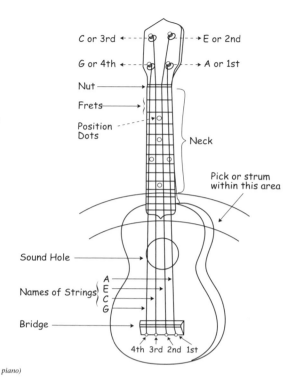

The songs in this book are arranged for ukuleles in C tuning. In this tuning, the individual strings from top (closest to your head) to bottom (closest to your feet) are tuned GCEA. One of the best things about the ukulele is that it is so easy to play. A lot of chords can be made with one or two fingers and many of the songs in this book can be played with three or four chords.

Uke C Tuning:

The easiest way to tune the ukulele is with a pitch pipe, matching the strings with the notes.

This corresponds to that famous melody:

Here are the notes on the keyboard.

To get the best sound out of your ukulele, make sure you are in tune. As soon as you are in tune, try holding the ukulele like the camper below.

For best results, the neck of your ukulele should be aimed at approximately 2:00. Press your uke against you with the middle of your forearm. Your strumming hand should naturally fall on top of the highest frets, not directly over the soundhole as first timers often think. Hold the neck of the uke between your thumb and first finger of your other hand so that your other fingers are free to move about the fretboard.

1 = Index finger
2 = Second finger
3 = Ring finger
4 = Pinky
0 = Open string (no fingers)

You make chords by putting different combinations of fingers on the fretboard. In this book, you'll find chord diagrams that show you where to put your fingers to get the right sound. The vertical lines in the diagrams represent strings and the horizontal lines represent frets. The numbers at the bottom of the chords shown below indicate what fingers to use.

C Chord

0   0   0   3

F Chord

2   0   1   0

G7 Chord

0   2   1   3

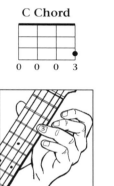
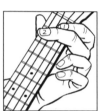

LOOKOUT

1. When pressing down the strings, use the tips of the fingers.
2. Always press down in the space between the frets, not on them.
3. Press the strings down to the fingerboard.
4. If you hear a buzz, you may not be pressing down hard enough or you may be too close to the fret.
5. Keep the thumb at the back of the neck, parallel to the frets.

Playing the ukulele requires two simultaneous actions. One is forming the chords. The second is strumming the strings. Most of the songs in this book can be strummed with the "common strum." This is basically a down-up motion with the pad of the thumb strumming downward on the strings and then the pad of the index finger coming up on them. (For more strumming techniques, refer to "Jumpin' Jim's Ukulele Tips 'N' Tunes.")

POISON IVY ALERT!
Stay away from plants that look like this. It can make you extremely itchy and cramp your ukulele style.

THE ANTS GO MARCHING

© 2000 Flea Market Music, Inc.
International Copyright Secured   Made in U.S.A.   All Rights Reserved

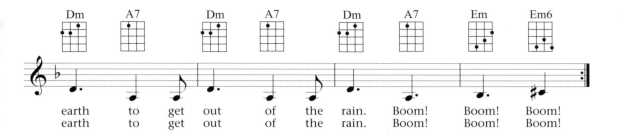

| earth | to | get | out | of | the | rain. | Boom! | Boom! | Boom! |
| earth | to | get | out | of | the | rain. | Boom! | Boom! | Boom! |

Additional Lyrics

3. The ants go marching three by three, hurrah, hurrah,
   The ants go marching three by three, hurrah, hurrah,
   The ants go marching three by three; the little one stops to climb a tree, and they
   all go marching down into the earth to get out of the rain. Boom! Boom! Boom!

4. The ants go marching four by four, hurrah, hurrah,
   The ants go marching four by four, hurrah, hurrah,
   The ants go marching four by four; the little one stops to shut the door, and they
   all go marching down into the earth to get out of the rain. Boom! Boom! Boom!

5. The ants go marching five by five, hurrah, hurrah,
   The ants go marching five by five, hurrah, hurrah,
   The ants go marching five by five; the little one stops to take a dive, and they
   all go marching down into the earth to get out of the rain. Boom! Boom! Boom!

6. The ants go marching six by six, hurrah, hurrah,
   The ants go marching six by six, hurrah, hurrah,
   The ants go marching six by six; the little one stops to pick up sticks, and they
   all go marching down into the earth to get out of the rain. Boom! Boom! Boom!

7. The ants go marching seven by seven, hurrah, hurrah,
   The ants go marching seven by seven, hurrah, hurrah,
   The ants go marching seven by seven; the little one stops to look to heaven, and they
   all go marching down into the earth to get out of the rain. Boom! Boom! Boom!

8. The ants go marching eight by eight, hurrah, hurrah,
   The ants go marching eight by eight, hurrah, hurrah,
   The ants go marching eight by eight; the little one stops to close the gate, and they
   all go marching down into the earth to get out of the rain. Boom! Boom! Boom!

9. The ants go marching nine by nine, hurrah, hurrah,
   The ants go marching nine by nine, hurrah, hurrah,
   The ants go marching nine by nine; the little one stops to drink and dine, and they
   all go marching down into the earth to get out of the rain. Boom! Boom! Boom!

10. The ants go marching ten by ten, hurrah, hurrah,
    The ants go marching ten by ten, hurrah, hurrah,
    The ants go marching ten by ten; the little one stops to say, "The end!"

THE BEAR WENT OVER THE MOUNTAIN

Traditional

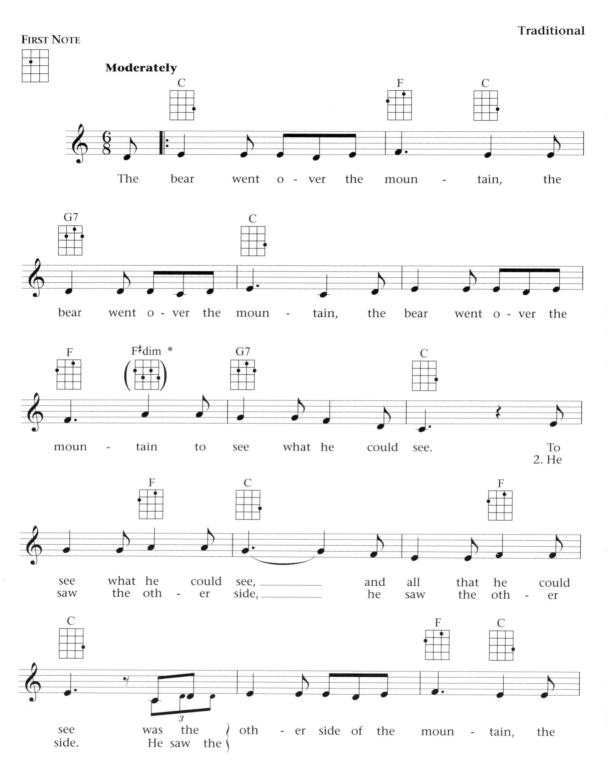

The bear went o - ver the moun - tain, the
bear went o - ver the moun - tain, the bear went o - ver the
moun - tain to see what he could see. To 2. He

see what he could see, _____ and all that he could
saw the oth - er side, _____ he saw the oth - er

see was the oth - er side of the moun - tain, the
side. He saw the

* Parenthetical chords: In this songbook you will find other instances of chords in parentheses.
These chords are not essential to the song, but do add flavor to the arrangement.

© 2000 Flea Market Music, Inc.
International Copyright Secured   Made in U.S.A.   All Rights Reserved

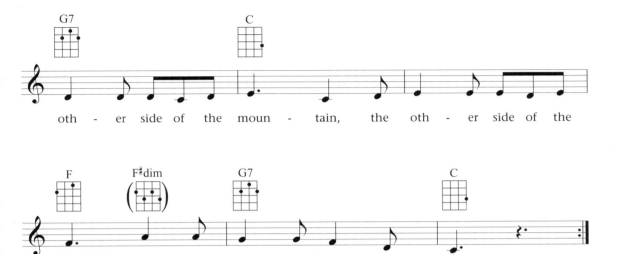

oth - er side of the moun - tain, the oth - er side of the

moun - tain was all that he could see.

BINGO

Traditional

FIRST NOTE

*Note: Each time a letter of BINGO is deleted in the lyric, tap your ukulele.

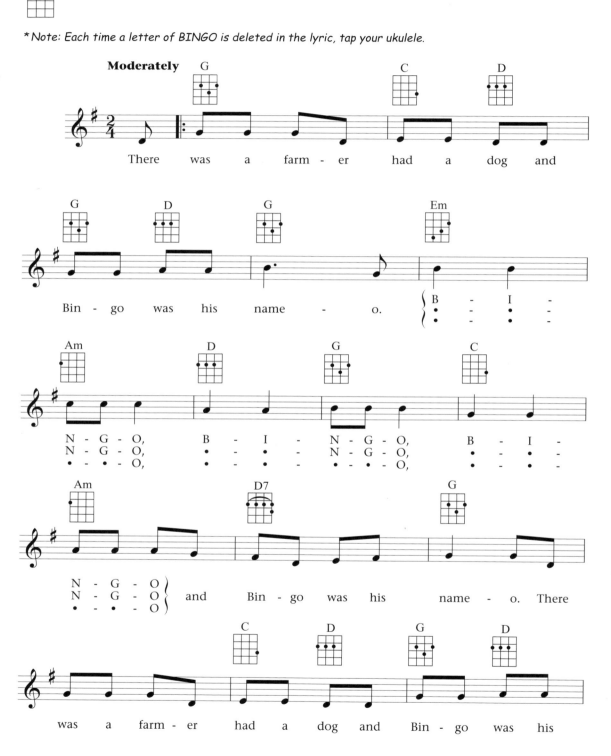

© 2000 Flea Market Music, Inc.
International Copyright Secured   Made in U.S.A.   All Rights Reserved

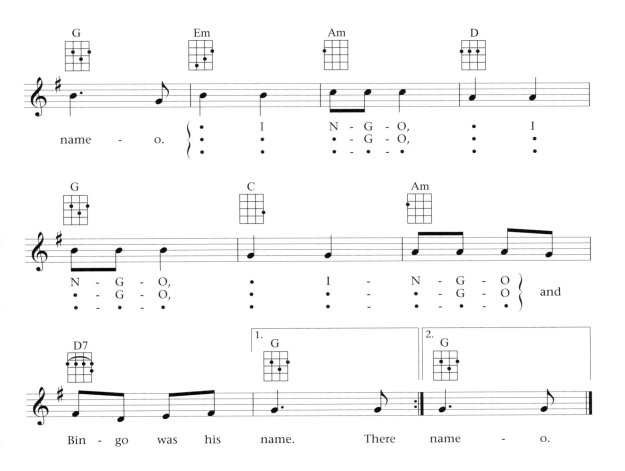

name - o. I N - G - O, I
N - G - O, I - N - G - O and
Bin - go was his name. There name - o.

CAMP UKULELE

Words and Music by
JIM BELOFF

© 2000 Flea Market Music, Inc.
International Copyright Secured   Made in U.S.A.   All Rights Reserved

CLEMENTINE

Traditional

1. In a cav - ern, in a can - yon, ex - ca -
2.-5. *See additional lyrics*

vat - ing for a mine, lived a min - er, for - ty -

nin - er, and his daugh - ter Clem - en - tine. Oh, my dar - ling, oh, my

dar - ling, oh, my dar - ling Clem - en - tine! You are

lost and gone for - ev - er, dread - ful sor - ry, Clem - en - tine!

© 2000 Flea Market Music, Inc.
International Copyright Secured   Made in U.S.A.   All Rights Reserved

Additional Lyrics

2. Light she was and, like a fairy,
   and her shoes were number nine;
   herring boxes, without topses,
   sandals were for Clementine.
   Chorus

3. Drove she ducklings to the water,
   every morning just at nine;
   hit her foot against a splinter,
   fell into the foaming brine.
   Chorus

4. Ruby lips above the water
   blowing bubbles soft and fine;
   but alas I was no swimmer,
   so I lost my Clementine.
   Chorus

THE CLIMBING SONG

Words and Music by
JIM BELOFF

FIRST NOTE

Moderately Fast

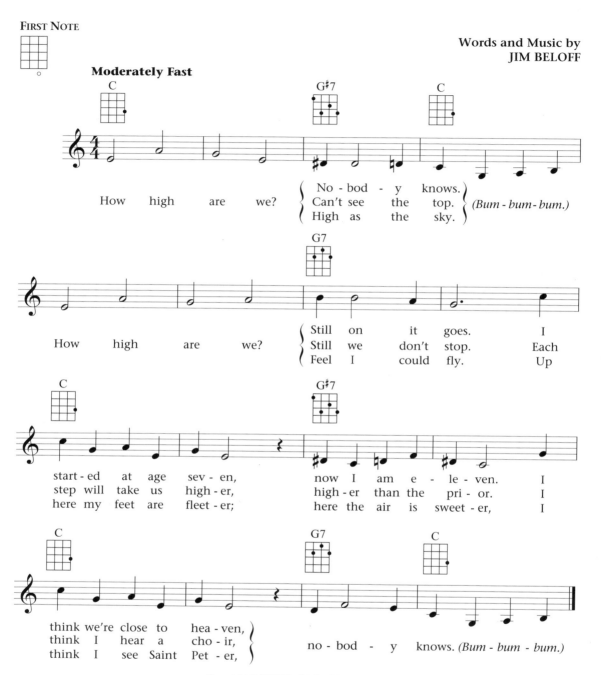

How high are we? { No - bod - y knows. / Can't see the top. *(Bum - bum - bum.)* / High as the sky. }

How high are we? { Still on it goes. I / Still we don't stop. Each / Feel I could fly. Up

start - ed at age sev - en, now I am e - le - ven. I
step will take us high - er, high - er than the pri - or. I
here my feet are fleet - er; here the air is sweet - er, I

think we're close to hea - ven, }
think I hear a cho - ir, } no - bod - y knows. *(Bum - bum - bum.)*
think I see Saint Pet - er, }

Copyright © 2000 Flea Market Music, Inc.
International Copyright Secured Made in U.S.A. All Rights Reserved

DOWN IN THE VALLEY

Traditional

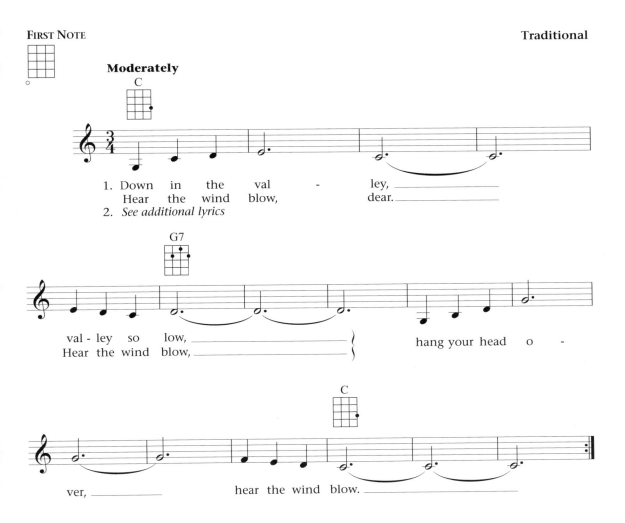

1. Down in the val - ley, dear.
   Hear the wind blow,
2. *See additional lyrics*

val - ley so low, hang your head o -
Hear the wind blow,

ver, hear the wind blow.

Additional Lyrics

2. Roses love sunshine, violets love dew;
   angels in heaven, know I love you.
   Know I love you dear, know I love you.
   Angels in heaven know I love you.

3. Build me a castle forty feet high,
   so I can see him as he rides by.
   As he rides by love, as he rides by.
   So I can see him as he rides by.

4. If you don't love me, love whom you please,
   throw your arms 'round me, give my heart ease.
   Give my heart ease, love, give my heart ease.
   Throw you arms 'round me, give my heart ease.

5. Write me a letter, send it by mail.
   Send it in care of Birmingham jail.
   Birmingham jail, love, Birmingham jail.
   Send it in care of Birmingham jail.

© 2000 Flea Market Music, Inc.
International Copyright Secured   Made in U.S.A.   All Rights Reserved

DOWN BY THE RIVERSIDE

Traditional

First Note

With Feeling

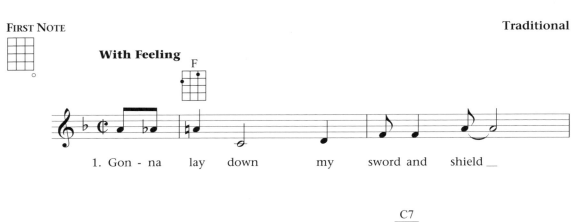

1. Gon - na lay down my sword and shield __

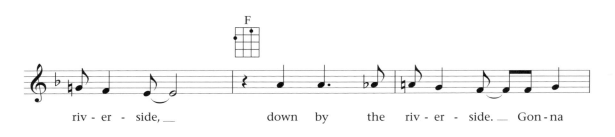

down by the riv - er - side, __ down by the

riv - er - side, __ down by the riv - er - side. __ Gon - na

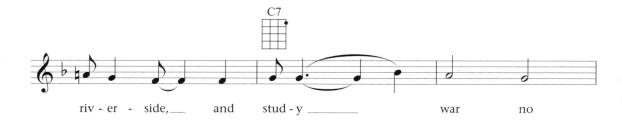

lay down my sword and shield __ down by the

riv - er - side, __ and stud - y __ war no

© 2000 Flea Market Music, Inc.
International Copyright Secured   Made in U.S.A.   All Rights Reserved

Chorus

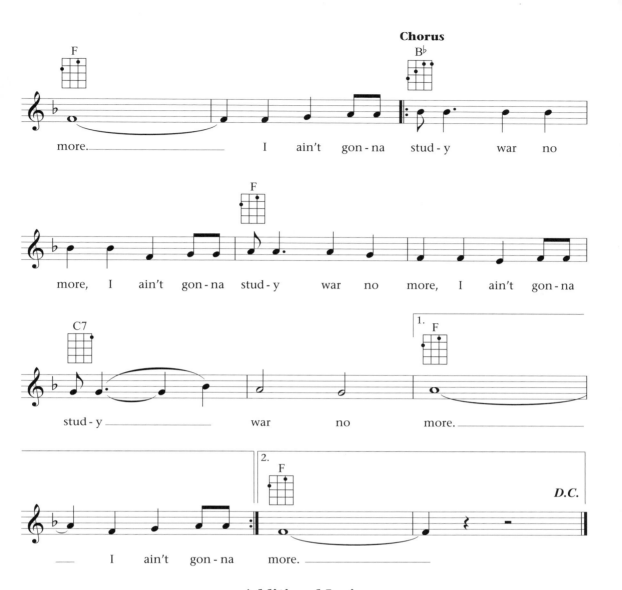

more. I ain't gon-na stud-y war no

more, I ain't gon-na stud-y war no more, I ain't gon-na

stud-y war no more.

I ain't gon-na more.

Additional Lyrics

2. I'm gonna join hands with everyone,
   down by the riverside, down by the riverside,
   down by the riverside,
   I'm gonna join hands with everyone,
   down by the riverside,
   and study war no more.

ERIE CANAL

Traditional

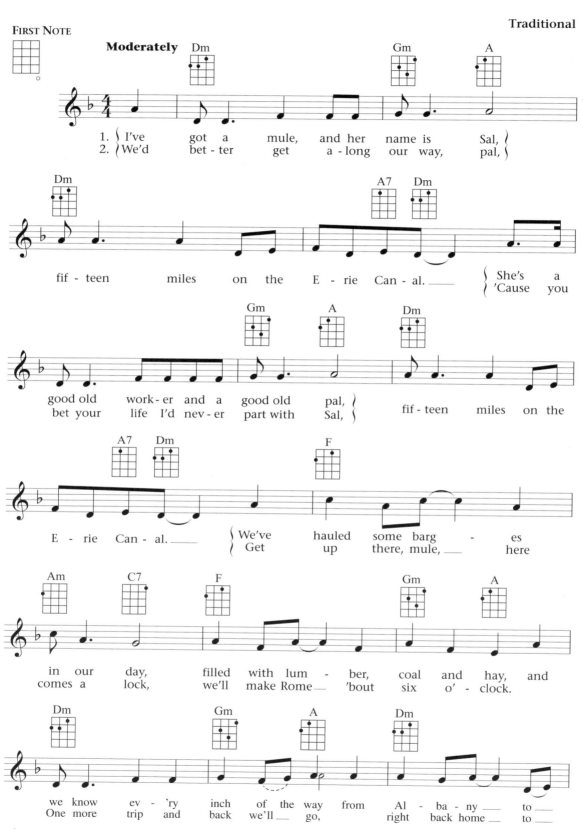

© 2000 Flea Market Music, Inc.
International Copyright Secured   Made in U.S.A.   All Rights Reserved

Chorus

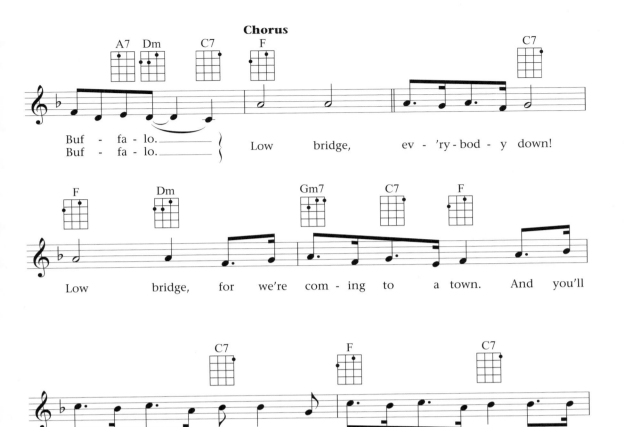

Buf - fa - lo._____ Buf - fa - lo._____ Low bridge, ev - 'ry - bod - y down!

Low bridge, for we're com - ing to a town. And you'll

al - ways know your neigh - bor, you'll al - ways know your pal, if you've

ev - er nav - i - gat - ed on the E - rie Can - al._____

Additional Lyrics

3. Oh, where would I be if I lost my pal?
Fifteen miles on the Erie Canal.
Oh, I'd like to see a mule as good as Sal
fifteen miles on the Erie Canal.

A friend of mine once got her sore,
now he's got a broken jaw,
'cause she let fly with her iron toe
and kicked him in to Buffalo.

4. You'll soon hear them sing all about my gal,
fifteen miles on the Erie Canal.
It's a darn fine ditty 'bout my darn mule Sal,
fifteen miles on the Erie Canal.

Oh, any band will play it soon,
darn fool words and darn'd fool tune.
You'll hear it sung before you go,
from Mexico to Buffalo.

GO DOWN, MOSES

Traditional

© 2000 Flea Market Music, Inc.
International Copyright Secured   Made in U.S.A.   All Rights Reserved

22

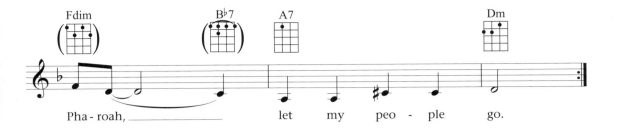

Pha - roah, _____ let my peo - ple go.

Additional Lyrics

3. The Lord told Moses what to do, let my people go.
    To lead the Hebrew children through, let my people go.
    Chorus

    O come along Moses, you'll not get lost, let my people go.
    Stretch out your rod and come across, let my people go.
    Chorus

    As Israel stood by the waterside, let my people go.
    At God's command it did divide, let my people go.
    Chorus

    When they reached the other shore, let my people go.
    They sang a song of triumph o'er, let my people go.
    Chorus

    Pharaoh said he'd go across, let my people go.
    But Pharaoh and his host were lost, let my people go.
    Chorus

    Jordan shall stand up like a wall, let my people go.
    And the walls of Jericho shall fall, let my people go.
    Chorus

    Your foes shall not before you stand, let my people go.
    And you'll possess fair Canaan's Land, let my people go.
    Chorus

    We need not always weep and mourn, let my people go.
    And wear these slavery chains forlorn, let my people go.
    Chorus

23

HAPPY TRAILS
(FROM THE TELEVISION SERIES, *THE ROY ROGERS SHOW*)

Words and Music by
DALE EVANS

Copyright © 1951, 1952 (Renewed 1979, 1980) by Paramount-Roy Rogers Music Company, Inc.
International Copyright Secured   All Rights Reserved

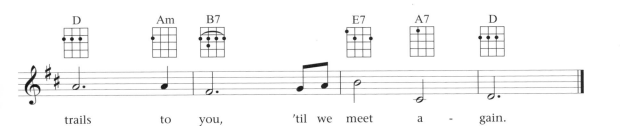

trails   to   you,   'til   we   meet   a   -   gain.

HELLO MUDDUH, HELLO FADDUH
(A LETTER FROM CAMP)

Words and Music by
ALLAN SHERMAN and LOU BUSCH

Copyright © 1963 (Renewed) WB MUSIC CORP. and BURNING BUSH MUSIC
All Rights Reserved   Used by Permission

Skin - ner? He got pto - maine pois - 'ning last night af - ter
Hard - y? They're a - bout to or - gan - ize a search - ing

din - ner. *(1st time only)* 2. All the Take me home, oh Mud - duh, Fad - duh
par - ty. Take me home, I prom - ise I will

take me home, I hate Gra - na - da; don't leave
not make noise, or mess the house with oth - er

1.

me out in the for - est, where I might get
boys. Oh please don't make me

2.

eat - en by a bear. stay, I've been here one whole day. Dear - est

Fad - duh, dar - ling Mud - duh, How's my pre - cious lit - tle

27

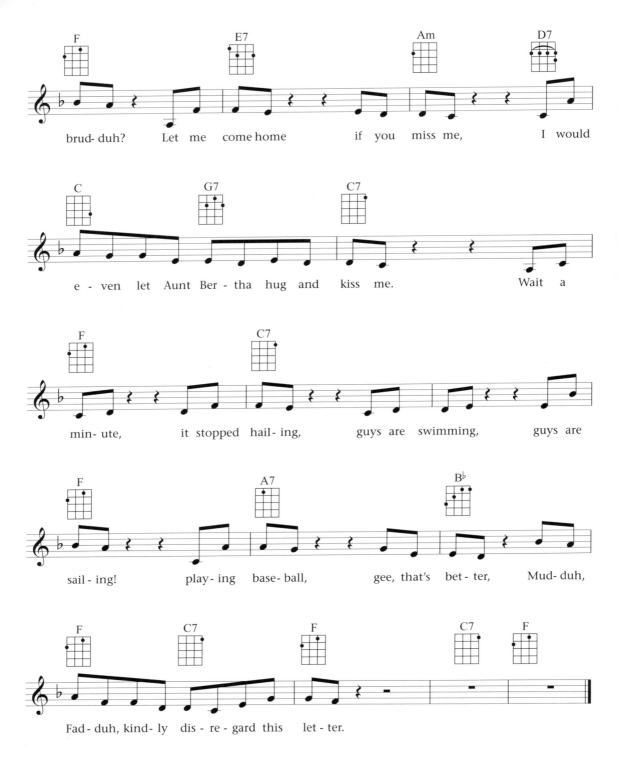

brud- duh? Let me come home if you miss me, I would

e - ven let Aunt Ber - tha hug and kiss me. Wait a

min- ute, it stopped hail- ing, guys are swimming, guys are

sail - ing! play- ing base- ball, gee, that's bet - ter, Mud- duh,

Fad - duh, kind- ly dis - re- gard this let - ter.

HE'S GOT THE WHOLE WORLD IN HIS HANDS

Traditional

FIRST NOTE

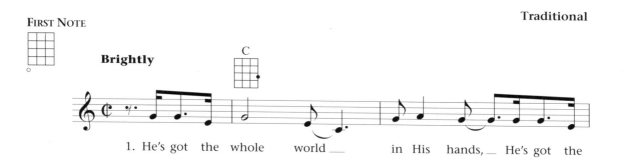

1. He's got the whole world ___ in His hands, ___ He's got the

whole world ___ in His hands, ___ He's got the whole world ___

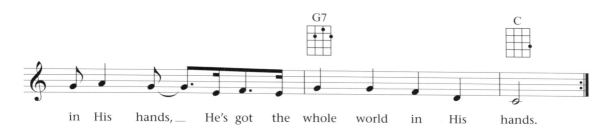

in His hands, ___ He's got the whole world in His hands.

Additional Lyrics

He's got a little ukulele, in His hands,
He's got a little ukulele, in His hands,
He's got a little ukulele, in His hands,
He's got the whole world in in His hands.

He's got you and me, brother, in His hands.
He's got you and me, sister, in His hands.
He's got you and me, brother, in His hands.
He's got the whole world in in His hands.

© 2000 Flea Market Music, Inc.
International Copyright Secured   Made in U.S.A.   All Rights Reserved

HOME ON THE RANGE

Traditional

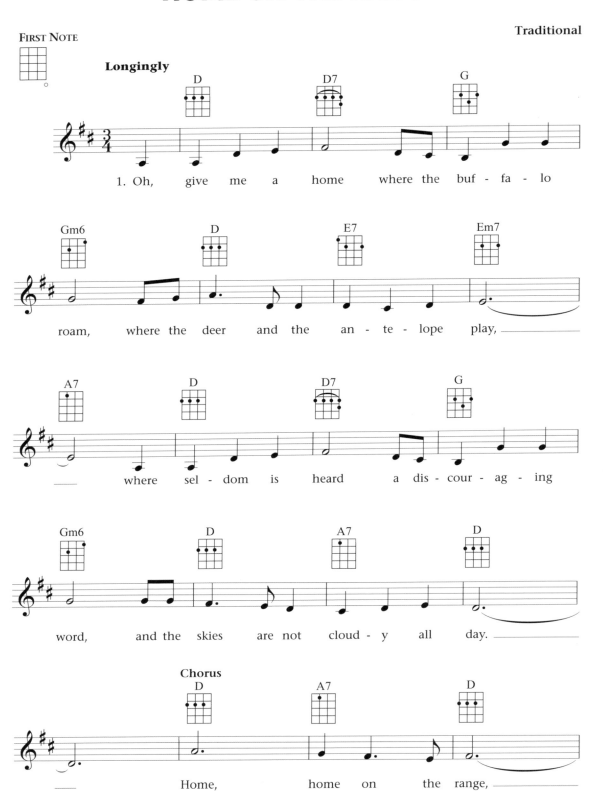

© 2000 Flea Market Music, Inc.
International Copyright Secured   Made in U.S.A.   All Rights Reserved

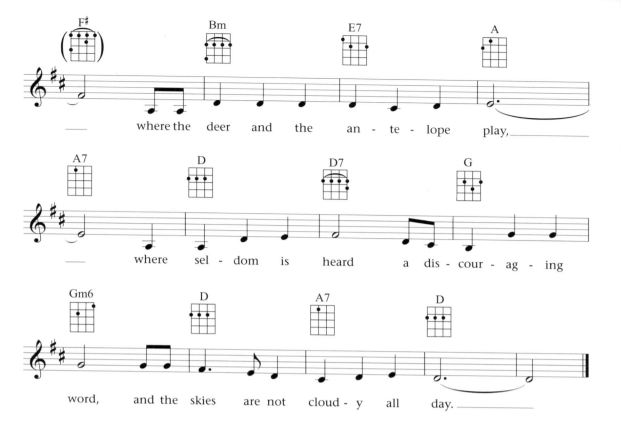

where the deer and the an - te - lope play,

where sel - dom is heard a dis - cour - ag - ing

word, and the skies are not cloud - y all day.

Additional Lyrics

2. Oh, give me a land where the bright diamond sand
   flows leisurely down the clear stream;
   where the graceful white swan goes gliding along
   like a maid in a heavenly dream.
   CHORUS

3. How often at night, when the heavens are bright
   with the light from the glittering stars,
   have I stood there amazed and asked as I gazed
   if their glory exceeds that of ours.
   CHORUS

4. Where the air is so pure, and the zephyrs so free,
   and the breezes so balmy and light,
   that I would not exchange my home on the range
   for all of the cities so bright.
   CHORUS

I'VE BEEN WORKING ON THE RAILROAD

Traditional

FIRST NOTE

I've been work-ing on the rail - road, all the live - long day;

I've been work-ing on the rail - road, just to pass the time a - way.

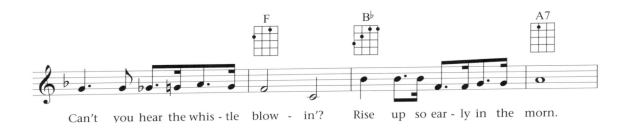

Can't you hear the whis-tle blow - in'? Rise up so ear-ly in the morn.

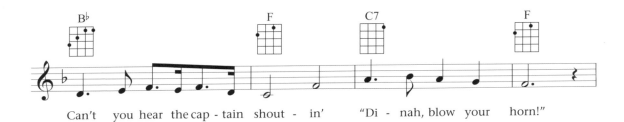

Can't you hear the cap-tain shout - in' "Di - nah, blow your horn!"

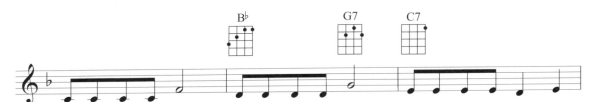

Di - nah, won't you blow, Di - nah, won't you blow, Di - nah won't you blow your

© 2000 Flea Market Music, Inc.
International Copyright Secured   Made in U.S.A.   All Rights Reserved

horn? _____ Di - nah, won't you blow, Di - nah won't you blow,

Di - nah won't you blow your horn? Some-one's in the kitch-en with Di - nah,

some-one's in the kitch-en I know, _____ some-one's in the kitch-en with

Di - nah strum-min' on the old ban - jo and sing-in' "Fee, fi,

fid - dle-ee - i - o, fee, fi, fid-dle-ee - i - o, _____

fee, fi, fid-dle-ee-i-o." Strum-min' on the old ban - jo.

33

KOOKABURRA

Traditional
Australia

FIRST NOTE

With a Lilt

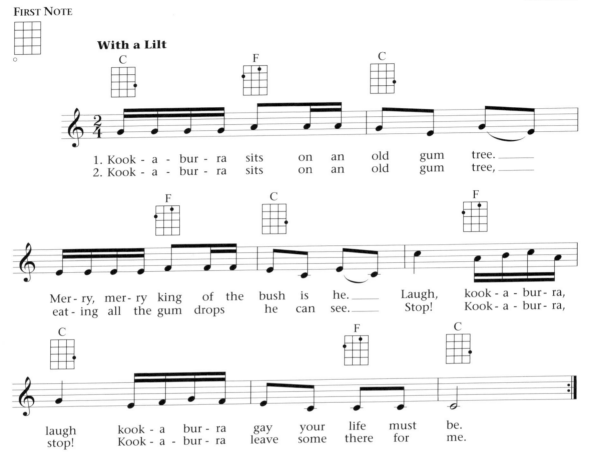

1. Kook - a - bur - ra   sits   on   an   old   gum   tree. ____
2. Kook - a - bur - ra   sits   on   an   old   gum   tree, ____

Mer - ry, mer - ry king   of   the   bush   is   he. ____   Laugh,   kook - a - bur - ra,
eat - ing all   the gum   drops   he   can   see. ____   Stop!   Kook - a - bur - ra,

laugh   kook - a - bur - ra   gay   your   life   must   be.
stop!   Kook - a - bur - ra   leave   some   there   for   me.

© 2000 Flea Market Music, Inc.
International Copyright Secured   Made in U.S.A.   All Rights Reserved

KUM-BAH-YAH

Traditional

FIRST NOTE

Slowly

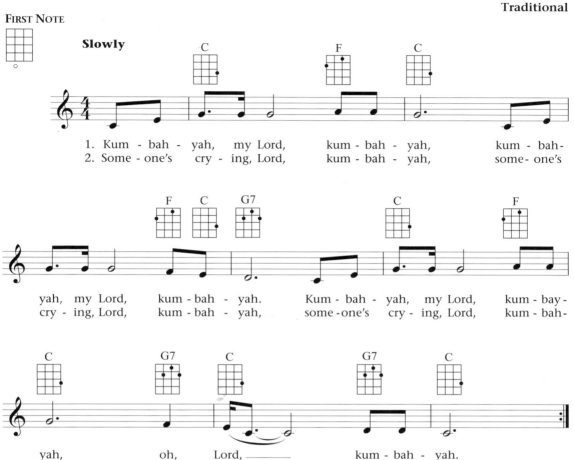

1. Kum - bah - yah, my Lord, kum - bah - yah, kum - bah -
2. Some - one's cry - ing, Lord, kum - bah - yah, some - one's

yah, my Lord, kum - bah - yah. Kum - bah - yah, my Lord, kum - bay -
cry - ing, Lord, kum - bah - yah, some - one's cry - ing, Lord, kum - bah -

yah, oh, Lord, _____ kum - bah - yah.
yah, oh, Lord, _____ kum - bah - yah.

Additional Lyrics

3. Someone's singing, Lord, kum-bah-yah...
4. Someone's praying, Lord, kum-bah-yah...

© 2000 Flea Market Music, Inc.
International Copyright Secured   Made in U.S.A.   All Rights Reserved

THE LION SLEEPS TONIGHT

New lyric and revised music by
GEORGE DAVID WEISS, HUGO PERETTI,
and LUIGI CREATORE

© COPYRIGHT 1961 FOLKWAYS MUSIC PUBLISHERS, INC.
Copyright Renewed 1989 by GEORGE DAVID WEISS, LUIGI CREATORE and JUNE PERETTI
Copyright Assigned to ABILENE MUSIC, INC., c/o
THE SONGWRITERS GUILD OF AMERICA
All Rights Reserved   Used by Permission

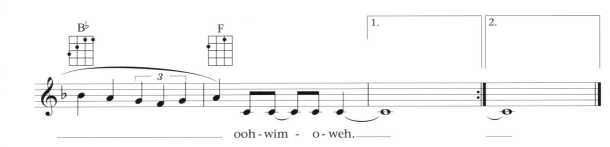

ooh - wim - o - weh.

MICHAEL, ROW THE BOAT ASHORE

Traditional

FIRST NOTE

Moderately

1. Mi - chael, row the boat a - shore, al - le - lu -
2.-5. *See additional lyrics*

ia! Mi - chael, row the boat a - shore, al - le - lu - ia!

Additional Lyrics

2. Michael's boat is a music boat, alleluia!
   Michael's boat is a music boat, alleluia!

3. Sister, help to trim the sail, alleluia!
   Sister, help to trim the sail, alleluia!

4. Jordan River is chilly and cold, alleluia!
   Chills the body, but not the soul, alleluia!

5. The river is deep and the river is wide, alleluia!
   Milk and honey on the other side, alleluia!

© 2000 Flea Market Music, Inc.
International Copyright Secured   Made in U.S.A.   All Rights Reserved

Greetings from Central Lake. Mich.

OH, SUSANNA

Words and Music by
STEPHEN FOSTER

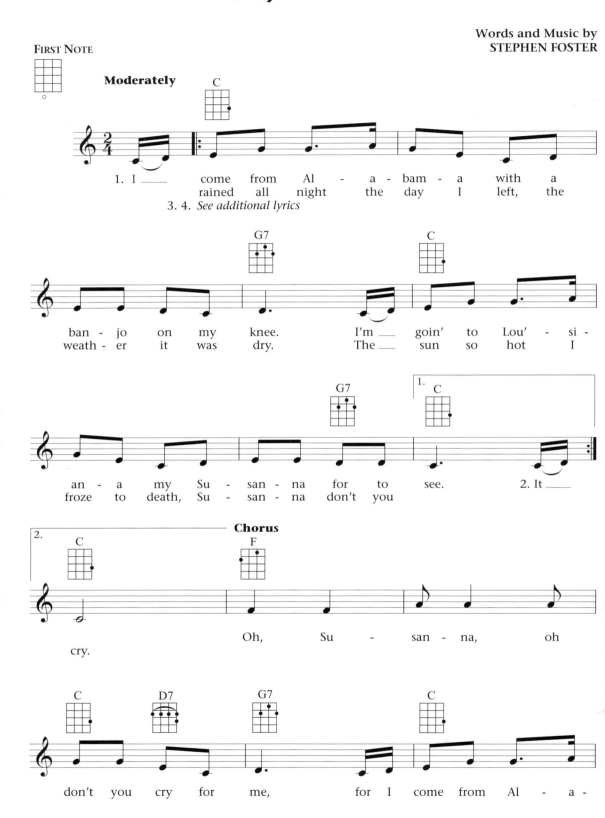

© 2000 Flea Market Music, Inc.
International Copyright Secured   Made in U.S.A.   All Rights Reserved

40

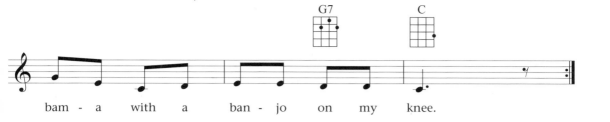

bam - a   with   a   ban - jo   on   my   knee.

Additional Lyrics

3. I had a dream the other night, when everything was still;
    I thought I saw Susanna a-coming down the hill.

4. The buckwheat cake was in her mouth, the tear was in her eye.
    Says I, "I'm coming from the South; Susanna, don't you cry!"

The banjo-shaped "Camp Uke" could be played
"on the beach, in a canoe, or in the woods"
according to a 1925 Lyon & Healy catalog.

ON TOP OF OLD SMOKY

Traditional

FIRST NOTE

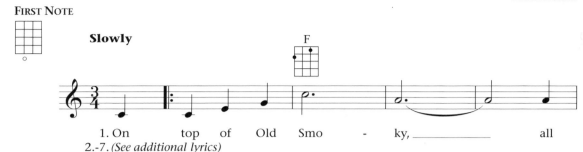

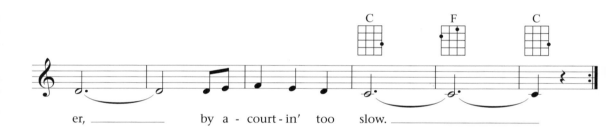

cov-ered with snow, _____ I lost my true lov -

er, _____ by a - court - in' too slow. _____

Additional Lyrics

2. Well, a-courting's a pleasure,
   and parting is grief.
   But a false-hearted lover
   is worse than a thief.

3. A thief he will rob you
   and take all you have.
   But a false-hearted lover
   will send you to your grave.

4. They'll hug you and kiss you
   and tell you more lies
   than the cross-ties on the railroad,
   or the stars in the skies.

5. They'll tell you they love you,
   just to give your heart ease.
   But the minute your back's turned,
   they'll court whom they please.

6. So come all you young maidens
   and listen to me.
   never place your affection
   on a green willow tree.

7. For the leaves they will wither
   and the roots they will die.
   And your true love will leave you,
   and you'll never know why.

© 2000 Flea Market Music, Inc.
International Copyright Secured   Made in U.S.A.   All Rights Reserved

ON TOP OF SPAGHETTI

Words and Music by
TOM GLAZER

FIRST NOTE

Moderately Fast

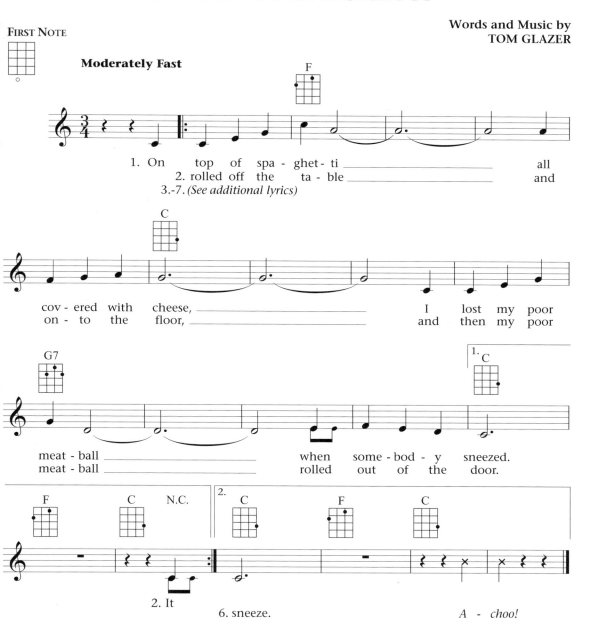

1. On top of spa-ghet-ti _____ all
2. rolled off the ta-ble _____ and
3.-7. (See additional lyrics)

cov-ered with cheese, _____ I lost my poor
on-to the floor, _____ and then my poor

meat-ball _____ when some-bod-y sneezed.
meat-ball _____ rolled out of the door.

2. It

6. sneeze.   A - choo!

Additional Lyrics

3. It rolled in the garden
   and under a bush,
   and then my poor meatball
   was nothing but mush.

4. The mush was as tasty
   as tasty could be,
   and early next summer,
   it grew into a tree.

5. The tree was all covered
   with beautiful moss;
   it grew lovely meatballs
   and tomato sauce.

6. So if you eat spaghetti
   all covered with cheese,
   hold onto your meatballs
   and don't ever sneeze. *A-choo!*

Copyright © 1963, 1965 by Songs Music Inc.
Copyright Renewed 1991
International Copyright Secured   All Rights Reserved

43

PUFF, THE MAGIC DRAGON

Words and Music by
PETER YARROW and LEONARD LIPTON

FIRST NOTE

Moderately

1. Puff, the mag - ic drag - on, lived by the
*2.-5. See additional lyrics

*3rd time, play verses 3 & 4
before proceeding to Chorus.

sea and frol - icked in the au - tumn mist in a land called Hon - a -

lee. Lit - tle Jack - ie Pa - per loved that ras - cal

Puff and brought him strings and seal - ing wax and oth - er fan - cy

Chorus

stuff. Oh! Puff, the mag - ic drag - on, lived by ___ the

Copyright © 1963 by PEPAMAR MUSIC CORP.
Copyright Renewed and Assigned to
SILVER DAWN MUSIC and HONALEE MELODIES
All Rights on behalf of HONALEE MELODIES Administered
Worldwide by CHERRY LANE MUSIC PUBLISHING COMPANY, INC.
All Rights Reserved   Used by Permission

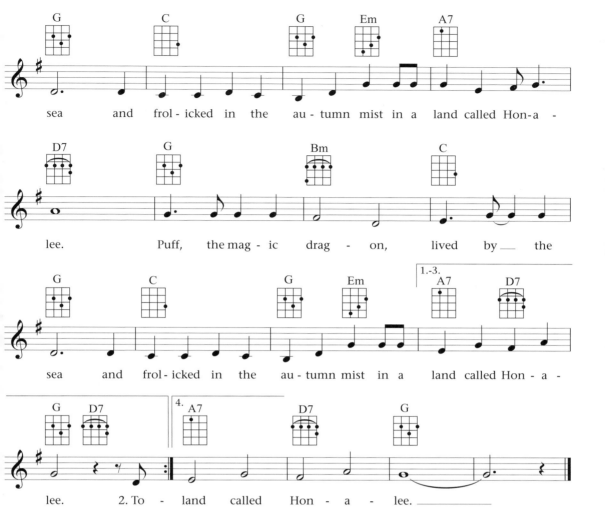

sea and frol - icked in the au - tumn mist in a land called Hon-a - lee. Puff, the mag - ic drag - on, lived by ___ the sea and frol - icked in the au - tumn mist in a land called Hon - a - lee. 2. To - land called Hon - a - lee. ___

Additional Lyrics

2. Together they would travel on a boat with billowed sail.
   Jackie kept a lookout perched on Puff's gigantic tail.
   Noble kings and princes would bow when e'er they came.
   Pirate ships would low'r their flags when Puff roared out his name. Oh!

3. A dragon lives forever, but not so little boys.
   Painted wings and giant rings make way for other toys.
   One gray night it happened, Jackie Paper came no more,
   and Puff that mighty dragon, he ceased his fearless roar.

4. His head was bent in sorrow, green tears fell like rain.
   Puff no longer went to play along the Cherry Lane.
   Without his lifelong friend, Puff could not be brave,
   so Puff that mighty dragon sadly slipped into his cave. Oh!

The Return of Puff

5. Puff, the Magic Dragon, danced down the Cherry Lane.
   He came upon a little girl, Julie Maple was her name.
   She'd heard that Puff had gone away, but that can never be,
   so together they went sailing to the land called Honalee.

45

RED RIVER VALLEY

Traditional

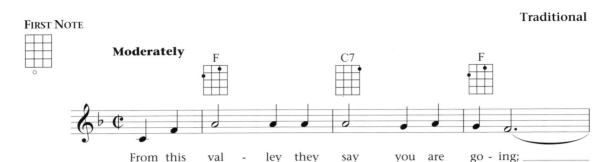

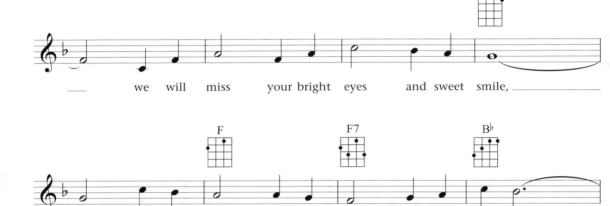

From this val - ley they say you are go - ing; ___ ___ we will miss your bright eyes and sweet smile, ___ ___ for they say you are tak - ing the sun -shine ___ ___ that has bright - ened our path - way a - while. ___

Additional Lyrics

2. Won't you think of this valley you're leaving?
Oh, how lonely, how sad it will be.
Oh, think of the fond heart you're breaking
and the grief you are causing me.

3. Come and sit by my side if you love me.
Do not hasten to bid me adieu,
but remember the Red River Valley
and the cowboy (cowgirl) that loves you so true.

© 2000 Flea Market Music, Inc.
International Copyright Secured   Made in U.S.A.   All Rights Reserved

RISE AND SHINE

Traditional

First Note

With Feeling

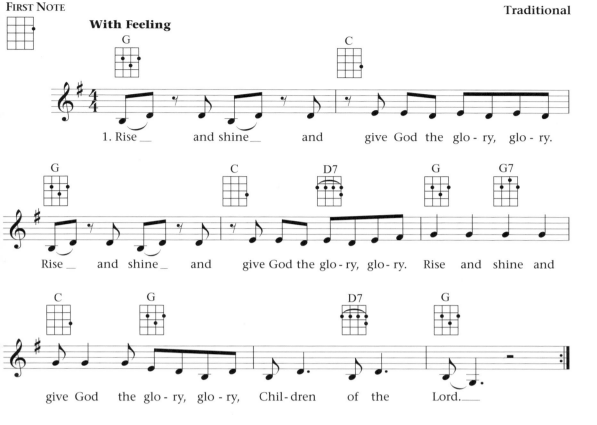

1. Rise __ and shine __ and give God the glo - ry, glo - ry.

Rise __ and shine __ and give God the glo - ry, glo - ry. Rise and shine and

give God the glo - ry, glo - ry, Chil - dren of the Lord. __

Additional Lyrics

2. The Lord said to Noah, "There's gonna be a floody, floody."
   The Lord said to Noah, "There's gonna be a floody, floody."
   Get your children out of the muddy, muddy!"
   Children of the Lord.

3. Noah, he built him, he built him an arky, arky.
   Noah, he built him, he built him an arky, arky.
   Made it out of hickory barky, barky,
   Children of the Lord.

4. The animals, they came on, they came on by twosy, twosy.
   The animals, they came on, they came on by twosy, twosy.
   Elephants and kangaroosy, 'roosy,
   Children of the Lord.

5. It rained and rained for forty daysy, daysy.
   It rained and rained for forty daysy, daysy.
   Nearly drove those animals crazy, crazy,
   Children of the Lord.

6. The sun came out and dried off the landy, landy.
   The sun came out and dried off the landy, landy.
   Everyone felt fine and dandy, dandy,
   Children of the Lord.

© 2000 Flea Market Music, Inc.
International Copyright Secured   Made in U.S.A.   All Rights Reserved

SHE'LL BE COMING 'ROUND THE MOUNTAIN

Traditional

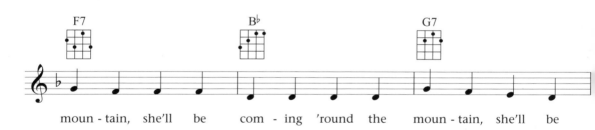

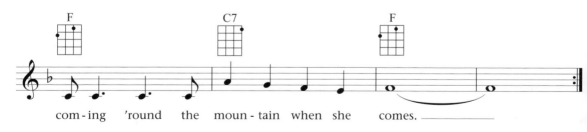

Additional Lyrics

2. She'll be driving six white horses when she comes, etc.

3. Oh, we'll all go down to meet her when she comes, etc.

© 2000 Flea Market Music, Inc.
International Copyright Secured   Made in U.S.A.   All Rights Reserved

SHENANDOAH

Traditional

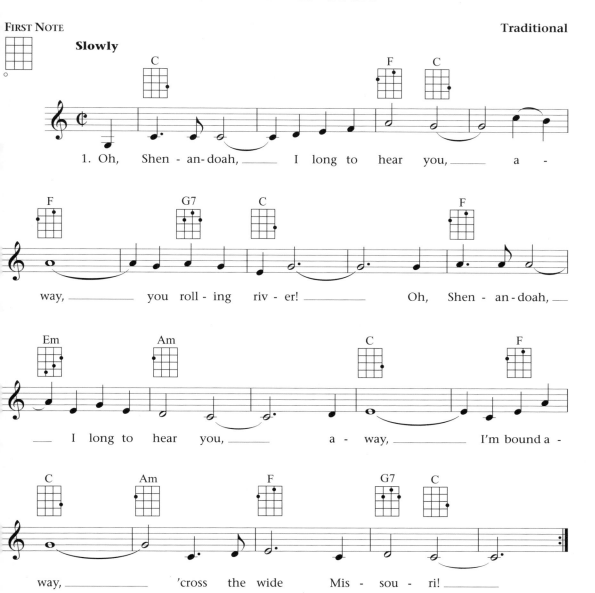

Additional Lyrics

2. Oh, Shenandoah, I love your daughter.
Away, you rolling river!
For her, I'd cross the rolling water.
Away, I'm bound away, 'cross the wide Missouri.

3. Oh, Shenandoah, I'm bound to leave you.
Away, you rolling river!
Oh, Shenandoah, I'll not deceive you.
Away, I'm bound away, 'cross the wide Missouri.

© 2000 Flea Market Music, Inc.
International Copyright Secured   Made in U.S.A.   All Rights Reserved

THE SLOOP JOHN B.

Bahamian Folk Song

© 2000 Flea Market Music, Inc.
International Copyright Secured   Made in U.S.A.   All Rights Reserved

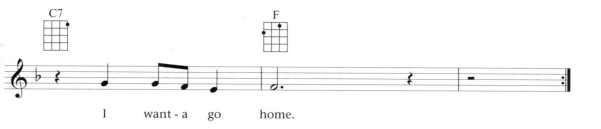

I want - a go home.

Additional Lyrics

CHORUS: (same chords as verse)
So hoist up the John B. sails.
See how the mainsail sets.
Send for the captain ashore, let me go home.
Let me go home, let me go home.
I feel so break up, I want to go home.

2. The first mate, oh, he got drunk,
   Broke up the people's trunk.
   Constable had to come and take him away.
   Sheriff Johnstone, please leave me alone.
   I feel so break up, I want to go home.
   Chorus

3. The poor cook, oh, he got fits,
   Throw away all of the grits.
   Then he took and eat up all of my corn.
   Let me go home, I want to go home.
   This is the worst trip I've ever been on.
   Chorus

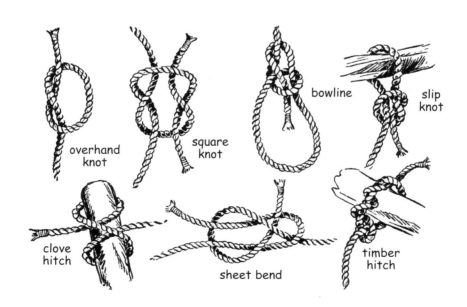

overhand knot

square knot

bowline

slip knot

clove hitch

sheet bend

timber hitch

SWING LOW, SWEET CHARIOT

Traditional

Swing low sweet char - i - ot, ___ com-in' for to car-ry me home; swing ___ low sweet char - i - ot, ___ com-in' for to car-ry me home.

I
If

looked o - ver Jor - dan and what did I see? ___
you get there be - fore I do, ___

Com-in' for to car - ry me home, a
com-in' for to car - ry me home, tell

© 2000 Flea Market Music, Inc.
International Copyright Secured   Made in U.S.A.   All Rights Reserved

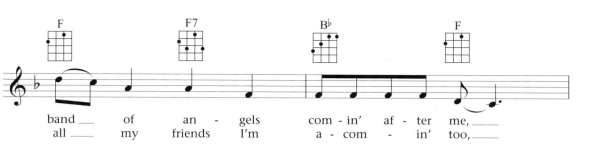

band __ of an - gels com - in' af - ter me, __
all __ my friends I'm a - com - in' too, __

1.

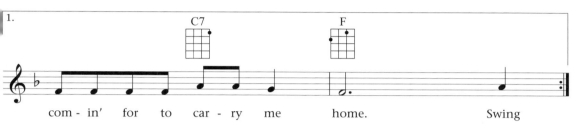

com - in' for to car - ry me home. Swing

2.

Com - in' for to car - ry me home.

SIMPLE GIFTS

Shaker Hymn

© 2000 Flea Market Music, Inc.
International Copyright Secured   Made in U.S.A.   All Rights Reserved

THIS OLD MAN

Traditional

First Note

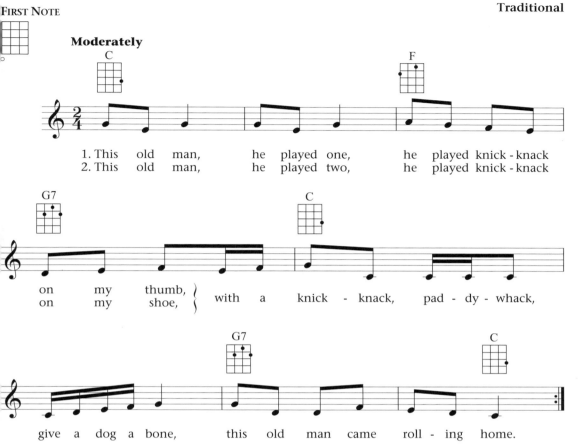

Moderately

1. This old man, he played one, he played knick-knack
2. This old man, he played two, he played knick-knack

on my thumb,
on my shoe, } with a knick - knack, pad - dy - whack,

give a dog a bone, this old man came roll - ing home.

Additional Lyrics

3. This old man, he played three,
   he played knick-knack on my knee.
   (Chorus)

4. This old man, he played four,
   he played knick-knack on my door.
   (Chorus)

5. This old man, he played five,
   he played knick-knack on my hive.
   (Chorus)

6. This old man, he played six,
   he played knick-knack on my sticks.
   (Chorus)

7. This old man, he played seven,
   he played knick-knack up to heaven.
   (Chorus)

8. This old man, he played eight,
   he played knick-knack on my gate.
   (Chorus)

9. This old man, he played nine,
   he played knick-knack on my vine.
   (Chorus)

10. This old man, he played ten,
    he played knick-knack over again.
    (Chorus)

© 2000 Flea Market Music, Inc.
International Copyright Secured   Made in U.S.A.   All Rights Reserved

TAKE ME OUT TO THE BALLGAME

Lyrics by JACK NORWORTH
Music by ALBERT VON TILZER

© 2000 Flea Market Music, Inc.
International Copyright Secured   Made in U.S.A.   All Rights Reserved

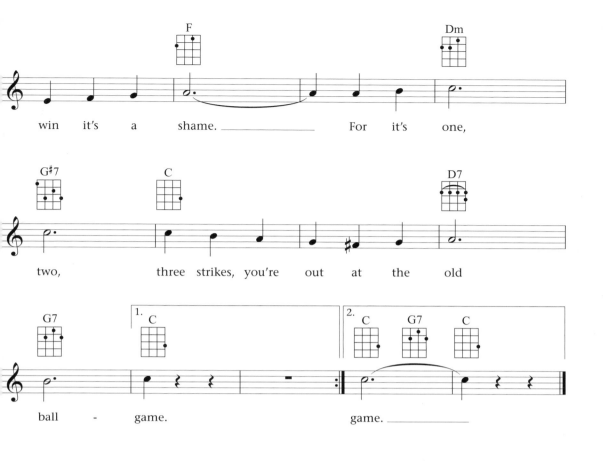

win it's a shame. _____ For it's one,

two, three strikes, you're out at the old

ball - game. game. _____

TELL ME WHY

Traditional

Moderately Slow

1. Tell _____ me why _____ the stars do
2. Be - cause God made _____ the stars to

shine, tell _____ me why _____ the
shine, be - cause God made _____ the

i - vy twines. Tell _____ me why _____ the
i - vy twine. Be - cause God made _____ the

skies are blue, and I will
skies so blue, be - cause God

tell you why I _____ love you.
made you, that's why I love you.

© 2000 Flea Market Music, Inc.
International Copyright Secured   Made in U.S.A.   All Rights Reserved

THE STORY OF THE UKULELE

The ukulele is the result of a happy meeting between two cultures. On August 23rd, 1879, a ship called the Ravenscrag from the Portuguese island of Madeira arrived in Honolulu harbor. One of the 419 Madeirans on board the ship was Joao Fernandez, who upon arrival proceeded to sing Portuguese songs of thanksgiving for the safe conclusion of a difficult, four month-long journey. The islanders who had come to welcome the foreigners were fascinated by the unique instrument Fernandez was playing. Known as the braguinha in Madeira, this simple four-string instrument was immediately embraced by the Hawaiians and promptly renamed ukulele. Pronounced "oo-koo-le-le," it was a composite of two Hawaiian words "uku" and "lele" which translate into "flea" and "jump" respectively. The name was inspired by watching a player's fingers skip up and down the fretboard, like little "jumping fleas."

Hawaiian royalty also played a major role in helping to popularize the ukulele. It was the favorite musical instrument of King David Kalakaua who learned to both play and make ukuleles. King Kalakaua's sister, the future Queen Lili'uokalani (who wrote many songs including the famous "Aloha Oe"), was also a great admirer of the ukulele.

In 1915, Hawaii invested in its own pavilion at the Panama Pacific Exposition in San Francisco in an early effort to promote the beauty of Hawaii and its culture. For the many thousands of attendees this was their first chance to see a hula dance and hear a ukulele. The investment paid off handsomely as the Mainland fell madly in love with all things Hawaiian, including the ukulele. All of a sudden, Hawaiian-themed sheet music, Hawaiian recordings, Mainland-made ukuleles and uke-playing entertainers were all the rage.

There was a second wave of popularity for the ukulele in the early '50s, thanks to Arthur Godfrey. As a result of his many TV shows (including "Arthur Godfrey and His Ukulele," a twice weekly, 15 minute show where Godfrey gave uke lessons), uke sales took off once again. Mario Maccaferri sold 9 million of his famous Islander plastic ukuleles as a result of an early endorsement by Godfrey. So big was the interest in the ukulele, that today it is unlikely that you can find anyone who was around during this era who didn't play a uke or have a friend or family member who did.

With the start of the new millennium it appears that the ukulele is enjoying yet another wave of popularity. After all of these years, the ukulele continues to charm new generations by being a wonderfully portable musical instrument that is easy and fun to play and, most importantly, seems to bring a smile to just about everyone.

THIS LAND IS YOUR LAND

Words and Music by
WOODY GUTHRIE

This land is your land, _____ this land is my land _____
_____ from Cal - i - for - nia _____ to the New York is - land.
_____ From the red - wood for - est _____ to the gulf stream wa - ters;
_____ this land was made for you and me. _____

Verses

(tacet)

1. As I was walk - ing _____ that rib - bon of
2. I've roamed and ram - bled _____ and I fol - lowed my
3. When the sun comes shin - ing _____ then I was

TRO –©– Copyright 1956 (Renewed) 1958 (Renewed) 1970 (Renewed) Ludlow Music, Inc., New York, New York
International Copyright Secured   Made in U.S.A.
All Rights Reserved Including Public Performance For Profit   Used by Permission

C

high - way _____ I saw a - bove me _____
foot - steps _____ to the spark - ling sands of _____
stroll - ing, _____ and the wheat - fields wav - ing, _____

C

_____ that end - less sky - way. _____ I saw be -
_____ her dia - mond des - erts _____ and all a -
_____ and the dust clouds roll - ing. _____ A voice was

F   **C**

low me _____ that gold - en val - ley, _____
round me _____ a voice was sound - ing: _____
chant - ing _____ as the fog was lift - ing, _____

G7   **C**

(tacet)

this land was made for you and me. _____ This land is

Additional Lyrics

4. In the squares of the cities, by the shadow of the steeples,
   in the relief office, I saw my people.
   And some were stumbling and some were wondering if
   this land was made for you and me.
   Chorus

5. As I went rambling that dusty highway,
   I saw a sign that said, "Private Property."
   But on the other side it didn't say nothing—
   that side was made for you and me.
   Chorus

6. Nobody living can ever stop me,
   as I go walking my freedom highway.
   Nobody living can make me turn back—
   this land was made for you and me.
   Chorus

VERY EARLY MORNING
(FROM THE MUSICAL, *ALL ABOUT CAMP*)

Words and Music by
JIM BELOF

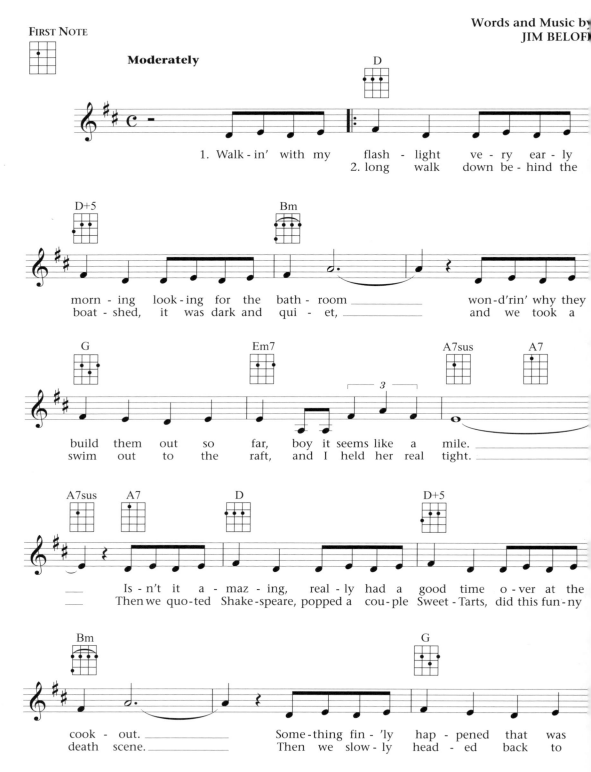

Lyrics:

1. Walk-in' with my flash-light ve-ry ear-ly morn-ing look-ing for the bath-room _____ won-d'rin' why they build them out so far, boy it seems like a mile. _____ Is-n't it a-maz-ing, real-ly had a good time o-ver at the cook-out. _____ Some-thing fin-'ly hap-pened that was

2. long walk down be-hind the boat-shed, it was dark and qui-et, _____ and we took a swim out to the raft, and I held her real tight. _____ Then we quo-ted Shake-speare, popped a cou-ple Sweet-Tarts, did this fun-ny death scene. _____ Then we slow-ly head-ed back to

© 1991 Flea Market Music, Inc.
International Copyright Secured   Made in U.S.A.   All Rights Reserved

All About Camp was originally produced at TADA!, Janine Nina Trevens, Artistic Director,
120 West 28th St., New York, NY 10001   PH: (212) 627-1732/FAX: (212) 243-6736

great   and it's mak - ing me smile._____   I met a
camp   and I kissed her good - night._____   I swear I

girl   to - night _____   and her   name is Jane. _____   We talked a - bout how
float - ed home _____   o - ver the din - ing hall._____   I   ran   a - round the

much   we   hat - ed   camp,   she gave me a   gum - wrap - per
soc - cer   field   five   times.   I   sang to a   teth - er _____

chain.   We sang the   same   dumb   songs _____   that we
ball.   The guys were   pump - ing   me _____   all a -

sing   each   year;   the couns - 'lors did the   same   old   In - di - an
bout   my   date.   I   told 'em that I   pro - mised   not   to

dance,   I said, "let's get a - way   from   here."   Then we took a
tell,   put 'em in a   fren - zied

WHEN THE SAINTS COME MARCHING IN

Traditional

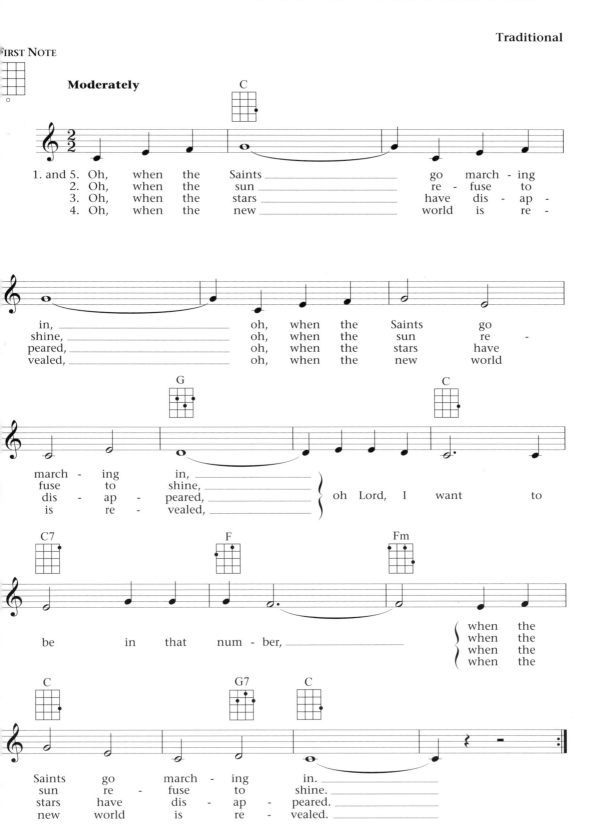

© 2000 Flea Market Music, Inc.
International Copyright Secured   Made in U.S.A.   All Rights Reserved

WALTZING MATILDA

Words by A. B. PATERSON
Music by MARIE COWAN

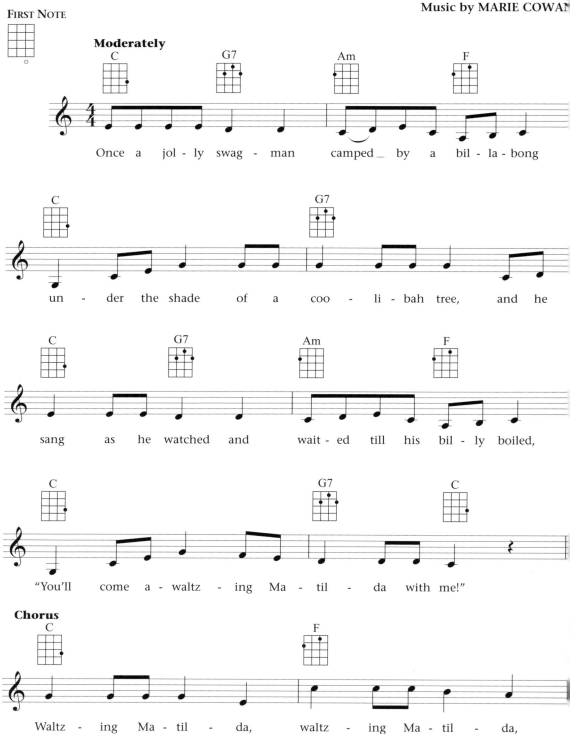

FIRST NOTE

Moderately

Once a jol - ly swag - man camped __ by a bil - la - bong

un - der the shade of a coo - li - bah tree, and he

sang as he watched and wait - ed till his bil - ly boiled,

"You'll come a - waltz - ing Ma - til - da with me!"

Chorus

Waltz - ing Ma - til - da, waltz - ing Ma - til - da,

Copyright © 1936 by Allan & Co. Prop. LTD. Melbourne, Australia
Copyright 1941 by Carl Fisher, Inc., New York
Copyright Renewed
All Rights Reserved

66

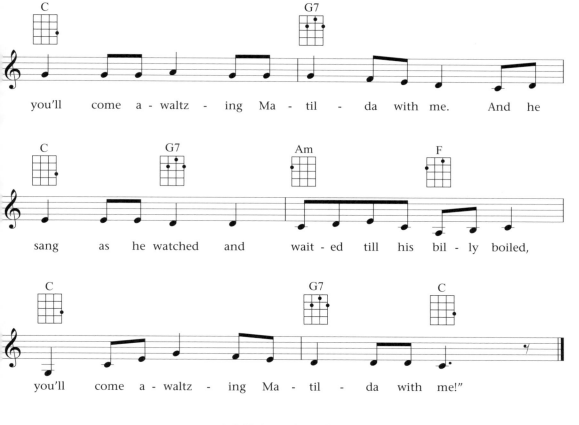

you'll come a - waltz - ing Ma - til - da with me. And he

sang as he watched and wait - ed till his bil - ly boiled,

you'll come a - waltz - ing Ma - til - da with me!"

Additional Lyrics

2. Down came a jumbuck to drink at the billabong,
   up jumped the swagman and grabbed him with glee.
   And he sang as he stowed that jumbuck in his tucker bag.
   "You'll come a-waltzing Matilda with me!"

3. Up rode the squatter, mounted on his thoroughbred.
   Down came the troopers, one, two, three,
   "Where's that jolly jumbuck you've got in your tucker bag?"
   "You'll come a-waltzing Matilda with me!"

4. Up jumped the swagman, sprang into the billabong.
   "You'll never catch me alive," said he.
   And his ghost may be heard as you pass by that billabong,
   "You'll come a-waltzing Matilda with me!"

THE WATER IS WIDE

British Folk Song

© 2000 Flea Market Music, Inc.
International Copyright Secured   Made in U.S.A.   All Rights Reserved

Additional Lyrics

. I leaned my back up against some young oak,
thinking he was a trusty tree.
But first he bended, and then he broke,
and thus did my false love to me.

4. I put my hand into some soft bush,
thinking the sweetest flower to find.
I pricked my finger to the bone,
and left the sweetest flower alone.

5. Oh, love is handsome and love is fine,
gay as a jewel when first it is new
But love grows old, and waxes cold,
and fades away like summer dew.

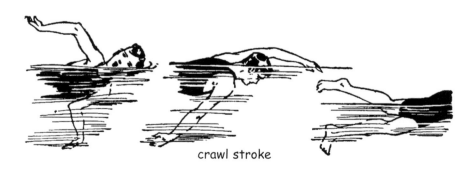

crawl stroke

YOU ARE MY SUNSHINE

Words and Music by
JIMMIE DAVIS and CHARLES MITCHELL

1. The oth - er night dear _____ as I lay
2. love you _____ and make you
3. once dear _____ you real - ly

sleep - ing _____ I dreamed I held you
hap - py. _____ If you will held on - ly
loved me, _____ and no one else could

in my arms. _____ When I a -
say the same, _____ but if you
come be - tween, _____ but now you've

woke dear _____ I was mis - tak - en _____
leave me _____ to love an - oth - er _____
left me _____ and love an - oth - er _____

_____ and I hung my head and
_____ you'll re - gret it all some
_____ you have shat - tered all my

© 1930 by Peer International Corporation
Copyright Renewed
International Copyright Secured   All Rights Reserved

Chorus

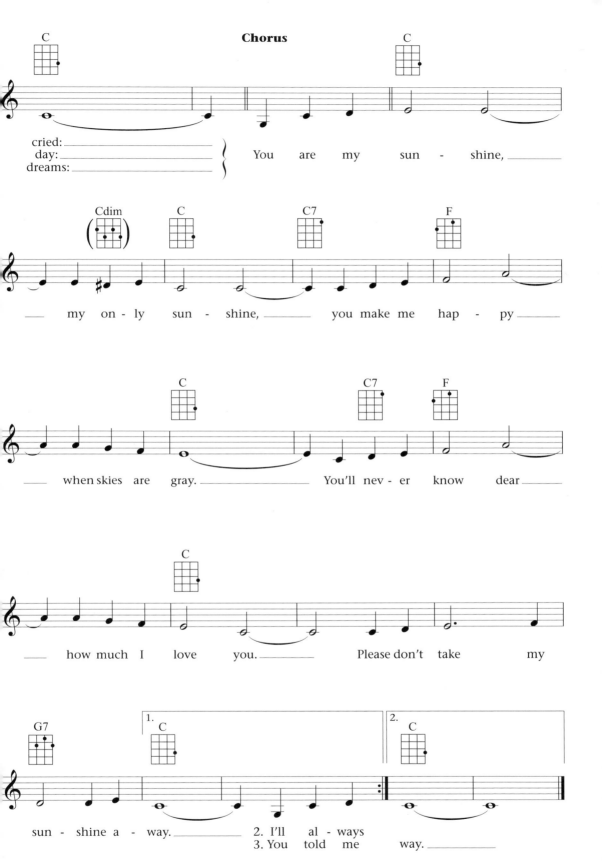

cried: _____
day: _____
dreams: _____

You are my sun - shine, _____ my on - ly sun - shine, _____ you make me hap - py _____ when skies are gray. _____ You'll nev - er know dear _____ how much I love you. _____ Please don't take my sun - shine a - way. _____

2. I'll al - ways
3. You told me way. _____

TAPS

FIRST NOTE

Slowly

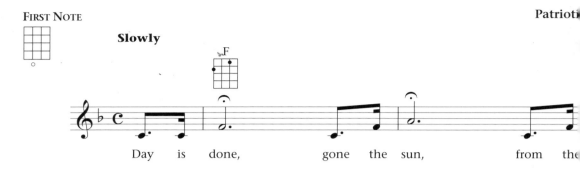

Day   is   done,   gone   the   sun,   from   the

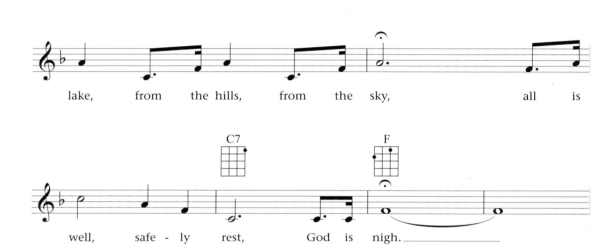

lake,   from   the   hills,   from   the   sky,   all   is

well,   safe - ly   rest,   God   is   nigh.

© 2000 Flea Market Music, Inc.
International Copyright Secured   Made in U.S.A.   All Rights Reserved